AN IDEAS INTO ACTION GUIDEBOOK

Communicating
Your Vision

IDEAS INTO ACTION GUIDEBOOKS

Aimed at managers and executives who are concerned with their own and others' development, each guidebook in this series gives specific advice on how to complete a developmental task or solve a leadership problem.

LEAD CONTRIBUTORS	Talula Cartwright
	David Baldwin
CONTRIBUTORS	Karen Bryson
	Paul Damiano
	George Houston
	Richard Hughes
	Gene Klann
DIRECTOR OF PUBLICATIONS	Martin Wilcox
EDITOR	Peter Scisco
ASSOCIATE EDITOR	Karen Mayworth
DESIGN AND LAYOUT	Joanne Ferguson
CONTRIBUTING ARTISTS	Laura J. Gibson
	Chris Wilson, 29 & Company

CCL No. 432
ISBN No. 1-882197-96-8

CENTER FOR CREATIVE LEADERSHIP
POST OFFICE BOX 26300
GREENSBORO, NORTH CAROLINA 27438-6300
336-288-7210
WWW.CCL.ORG / PUBLICATIONS

AN IDEAS INTO ACTION GUIDEBOOK

Communicating Your Vision

Talula Cartwright and David Baldwin

Center for
Creative
Leadership

NORTH AMERICA EUROPE ASIA

www.ccl.org

This series of guidebooks draws on the practical knowledge that the Center for Creative Leadership (CCL®) has generated, since its inception in 1970, through its research and educational activity conducted in partnership with hundreds of thousands of managers and executives. Much of this knowledge is shared—in a way that is distinct from the typical university department, professional association, or consultancy. CCL is not simply a collection of individual experts, although the individual credentials of its staff are impressive; rather it is a community, with its members holding certain principles in common and working together to understand and generate practical responses to today's leadership and organizational challenges.

The purpose of the series is to provide managers with specific advice on how to complete a developmental task or solve a leadership challenge. In doing that, the series carries out CCL's mission to advance the understanding, practice, and development of leadership for the benefit of society worldwide. We think you will find the Ideas Into Action Guidebooks an important addition to your leadership toolkit.

Table of Contents

7   Why You Need a Vision

7   What a Vision Is

10   The Leader's Role

21   Examples of Communicating a Vision

23   Meeting Resistance

26   Last Words

27   Suggested Readings

27   Background

28   Key Point Summary

A vision has to be shared in order to do what it is meant to do: inspire, clarify, and focus the work of your organization. One part of your job as a leader is to create commitment to your organization's vision. In order to do this, you have to communicate the vision effectively. In this guidebook we suggest many ways to communicate a vision. We also discuss how to deal with a resistant audience and what to do in the event that you yourself are resistant. You'll learn how to communicate a vision to others in ways that will help them understand it, remember it, and then go on to share it themselves.

Why You Need a Vision

Leaders in today's organizations face issues of growth, change, customization, globalization, and technology that force them to create new pathways toward success and sustainability. But a newly blazed strategic trail cannot itself create the focus, the underlying tactics, and the foresight necessary for long-term growth and deep impact. As Richard Hughes and Kate Beatty point out in *Becoming a Strategic Leader,* many organizations that falter have failed to effectively communicate their strategies. Employees do not understand their role in implementing the organization's mission and strategy. Leaders can adopt many tactics for coordinating messages and creating alignment among employees, whether at the unit, team, or organizational level. One effective tactic is to transmit strategic intent through a vision—an imagined or discerned future state that clearly captures the organization's direction and defines its destination.

What a Vision Is

A vision describes some achievement or some future state that the organization will accomplish or realize. It inspires, clarifies, and focuses the work of an organization for a significant time. A vision differs from goals, which express the steps of a plan for accomplishing an objective. A vision differs from a mission statement, which explains an organization's reasons for existence or for seeking its objectives.

Henry Ford's vision was a car that families could afford. Steve Jobs dreamed that aesthetically pleasing, easy-to-use

Understanding a Vision

Take a moment to reflect on your organization's vision. Use the following questions to focus your thoughts and to tap into your impressions about the vision.

- What is your organization's vision?

_____

_____

- Who created that vision for your organization?

_____

_____

- What importance do you place on the vision?

_____

_____

- How believable is it?

_____

_____

- What would you change about it?

_____

_____

The following characteristics define an effective vision. How does your organization's vision compare?

- imaginable—creates an accessible picture of the future

_____

- inspiring—ignites desire and personal connection to values (see Vision and Values worksheet on pages 12–13)

_____

- realistic—is achievable, with focused direction and distinguishable outcomes

_____

- flexible—offers space to grow, adapt, and develop

_____

- clear—is easily communicated and understood

_____

- compelling—moves people to action

_____

personal computers would have mass appeal and unleash popular creativity. Whatever your organization's vision may be, communicating that vision is a unique challenge. Employees may disagree about organizational values, or they may be unwilling to change or to be influenced in a particular direction. They may misunderstand the leader's intent or have trouble imagining the future state expressed in the vision. Effective communication of the vision is vital.

While there are distinctions to be made between vision, mission, and goals, the strategies and techniques for communication are applicable to all three. Throughout this guidebook, we will be less concerned with the distinctions and more concerned with the communication.

The Leader's Role

One part of a leader's job is to create commitment to and alignment with the organization's picture of future success. Communicating the vision throughout the organization is essential to moving the organization forward.

In order to inspire commitment to a vision, a leader needs to have an effective way to communicate it. Presumably, the leader supports the vision and can draw on his or her personal passion and professional commitment and credibility to be dynamic in presenting it to others. David Campbell, Senior Fellow at the Center for Creative Leadership, says that leaders who are perceived to be dynamic have a passion about something and speak about it often. Leaders should be this dynamic about the vision. They should be passionate about it, and they should speak about it often. Many people in an organization attribute its vision to the people in leadership roles. If leaders stop talking about the vision, it becomes more difficult to see. To keep the vision alive at one organization, the executive team utilizes an on-site video studio to record components of the vision. The recording is electronically distributed to managers around the globe and used as a platform to communicate and receive feedback from their direct reports in fulfillment of the organization's vision.

You can never communicate too much. Treat every communication effort as though it is your most important attempt at getting the message out. People may not hear it the first time around, and when they finally do hear it, they are likely to consider that the first time you have said anything about it. This is especially true when a leader introduces a new vision. People need time and opportunities to hear it, to separate the message from the noise of change. It takes more than one memo or speech to capture attention and build support. Intersperse the vision throughout regular conversations, be dynamic, and be intentional about continuously communicating.

Stories

Stories give life to a vision and help people see it clearly and remember it. Stories give integrity to the vision by grounding it in common values and truths. The telling of stories creates trust and captures the heart and mind of the audience. Stories establish common ground between the teller (the leader with a vision, in this case) and the audience (the other leaders, managers, employees, stakeholders, customers, and others associated with the organization). A story is a powerful tool for disseminating a vision; people share the story with others, creating a ripple effect.

In his book, *Managing Transitions: Making the Most of Change*, William Bridges explains his vision by using the ancient story of

Vision and Values

A vision statement typically expresses an ideal, and it is often connected to the organization's traditional values. Values are beliefs that should be reflected in the organization's behavior as well as in its policies and formal practices—for example, how it treats its employees, stakeholders, and customers; how it handles conflict and change; and how it encourages innovation and entrepreneurs. In some organizations there may be a difference between espoused values (stated values) and expressed values (values in action).

What are three of the most apparent values supported by your organization, based on the behaviors you observe?

1. _____

2. _____

3. _____

Review your answers in the Understanding a Vision worksheet on pages 8–9. How do the three values you listed connect to your organization's vision?

_____

_____

_____

Now think about your role as a leader in your organization with expressed values and a vision, and answer the following questions.

- How do you communicate through your actions your passion and enthusiasm for your organization's vision and for your role in achieving that vision?

_____

_____

- What obstacles are in the way of communicating your organization's vision?

_____

_____

- What can you do to surmount those obstacles? What new behavior can you model for others? What new actions can you take? How can you communicate the vision differently? To whom can you communicate?

_____

_____

- Who can give you support and feedback on your efforts to act on the organization's vision and communicate it to others?

_____

_____

Moses leading the Israelites out of Egypt. The story and its lessons are familiar, which makes it an excellent tool for motivating and inspiring his readers to embrace and champion his metaphor for change, its emotional fallout, and what needs to happen to move people from resistance to support.

Stories galvanize people around a cause and give them confidence as they move forward in the face of uncertainty. As tools for communicating a vision, Stephen Denning calls them springboard stories. In his work he talks about how executives at World Bank use stories to communicate the visions of the projects it funds.

Story Maker Exercise

Do you have a story associated with your personal vision or with the vision of your organization? You can probably put one together from small incidents you have seen or heard about. Make notes about how people in your organization live and act out the organization's vision. To make a story about your personal vision, think about what excites or satisfies you about how it connects to what you do every day.

The Elevator Speech

Stories are powerful, dynamic, and absolutely necessary for communicating a vision. Leaders do not always have the time or opportunity to tell them as often as they might like or need to, but that doesn't mean they shouldn't try to communicate the vision briefly, clearly, and with conviction at any opportunity. Enter the elevator speech—a concise and convincing statement that communicates the vision in the amount of time you have during a typical elevator ride. You must convey your message in a sentence or two at the most. Practice often and be prepared. Your elevator speech should sound natural and carry a sense of excitement and urgency.

Politicians are masters of these mini speeches. They live in the world of the seven-second sound bite. To thrive in that environment, they quickly learn to distill a position or a policy into a short phrase and use it to work a room—communicating a vision, building acceptance for their view, and spurring action among their supporters. The politician's policies and positions may be complex and detailed, but the vision for what things would look like if voters adopted them can be clear, simple, and passionate.

Leaders have similar opportunities to communicate their visions, especially with their employees and other stakeholders: a few minutes at the water cooler or in line at the cafeteria, a quick visit to the mail room or customer-service department, a company celebration, even a walk through the parking lot at the end of the workday. Like a politician, a leader should prepare for (and can create) these opportunities. The message may be short, but the impact over time and by repetition is exponential. Think, for example, about Verizon's "Can you hear me now?" It boasts about comprehensive mobile phone coverage and leaves a lingering memory of Verizon's vision of high customer satisfaction with its product.

Media Maven

In an instant-access, always-on wi-fi world of Treos and Blackberries, tried-and-true communication channels and tactics such as posters and business card reminders sound quaint, a relic of another time. Madison Avenue knows better. The more channels you open, the better your chances of communicating. Not every method works with everybody. Your organization's vision should be out front on its Web site, even if some people never look at a Web page. The ones who do will see it there, and you can reach the others with other methods.

Use pithy reminders wherever you can put them: on coffee mugs, T-shirts, letterhead, computer screensavers, luggage tags, pencils, file cabinet magnets, suggestion box prizes, notepads, and whatever else you can think of that will keep the message first and foremost in the minds of your employees, stakeholders, and customers. You can even embed the vision in your organization's performance and leadership development activities so that employees can associate their personal goals with the organization's future success.

To use all these media effectively, state the vision briefly. Revisit your elevator speech and imagine how to present that in other venues. People remember small phrases, even years after advertisers stop using them. Slogans like "Fly the friendly skies," "I'd like to teach the world to sing," "You deserve a break today," "Reach out and touch someone," and "I can't believe I ate the whole thing" are part of the common language, associated with specific products and even memories.

If you think about it, communicating a vision is really like making a sales pitch. You want people in the organization to believe the vision and to pass it on to others. You want it to be infectious, viral—to reach what Malcolm Gladwell has called the tipping point. Advertisers know all about and capitalize on our human need to belong to something bigger than ourselves.

Some leaders feel embarrassed or uneasy about the selling that is needed to communicate a vision. Even when it comes to their personal visions for success, some leaders feel uncomfortable promoting ideas because they are uncomfortable promoting themselves. But as a leader representing a vision, you are at the front of the curve. You are an early adopter. You already support the vision, but others may not even know enough about it to see it, much less support it. It is part of your job to inform and persuade.

Another effective strategy for communicating your vision is to make it personal, to engage others in one-on-one conversations. Personal connections are extraordinarily effective conduits for communication. They give leaders opportunities to transmit information, receive feedback, build support, and create energy around the vision. A leader's ability to develop these relationships requires skill at communicating a compelling and clear vision of the future. As Hughes and Beatty point out, when an organization understands where it is and where it wants to go, employees are more apt to join in on the journey and champion the cause.

As an example, consider the vision of "No child left behind" championed by President George W. Bush and later set into policy by Congress. Consider how that idea has been communicated along the education chain through links of personal connections. During a faculty meeting where a new curriculum initiative is introduced, a school principal might say, "Since we're committed to leaving no child behind, let's look at this new method to see if it might be useful for struggling students." Later, in response to a parent complaining about the difficulty his child is having with an assignment, a teacher might say, "Well, we're committed to leaving no child behind, and that certainly includes your daughter. Let's take a closer look at this situation."

Leaders can inspire themselves and others by tapping into their personal visions. Someone with a personal vision of leadership that includes serving others so that more caring and appreciation can be brought into the world can inject the core of that vision into conversations about conflict, influence, power, strategy,

Sprinkler System

- Think of your most recent conversations. How could you have inserted a mention of your organization's vision?

- Think about your own personal vision of leadership. How could you have inspired others by mentioning it to them?

empowerment, and many other leadership topics. Just a mention, in the context of personal relationships, can inform others and inspire them to think of the purpose and vision for their own leadership. Just as important, it keeps that particular leader inspired and aware of his or her own vision and invites rededication to it.

Other Ways

Stories, brief statements, channel variety, and personal connections are not the only means you have for communicating your vision. Here are some more suggestions for continuously and dynamically painting a picture of the future.

Draw a crowd. Identify key players, communicators, stakeholders, and supporters throughout the organization who will motivate others to listen, reflect on, and be engaged with the vision.

Map your ground. Create a formal communication strategy (like an advertising campaign, for example) and give a team the power and resources to implement it. Put a team in place to educate new staff.

Go outside. Communicate to external customers, partners, and vendors with catalogs, invoices, announcements, and other statements.

Keep to the sunny side. Stay positive about the vision. Pass along positive gossip; correct misinterpretations. People are going to talk. You have to decide what you want them to talk about.

Be everywhere your message can be. Visit different locations in your organization, whether that means a trip down to the mail room or a flight to the other side of the world. Make your presence known on your organization's intranet. Create a blog. Be the visible ambassador of your organization's vision, the champion of its success.

Make it meaningful. Sponsor contests and celebrations that encourage employees to own a part of the vision. Help them create the future, not wait for it.

Make memories. Create metaphors, figures of speech, and slogans, and find creative ways to use them. Write a theme song or a memorable motto.

Get loopy. Build continual feedback into the process of communicating your vision. Pay attention to what you put into the loop. Listen carefully to what comes back. Adjust, adapt, and remain flexible.

You are here. Use visual aids and updates to keep everyone aware of the progress you are making toward your vision. Create a vision GPS, but don't just give out maps. Guide the expedition.

Mind the gap. Explicitly and quickly address vision inconsistencies. Resistance to change may not be the issue—it may be that people have not heard your message or have misunderstood it. Be patient, move forward, and bring them along.

Notice the good deed. Reward behavior and actions that demonstrate and reflect the vision. Create curiosity and reward involvement.

KISS and tell. Remember the old acronym: *Keep It Short and Simple.* A statement of your vision should be clear, sensible, easy to understand, and easy to pass on.

See how the other half lives. Imagine that your employees are customers. Give them the message you want them to hear. Help them see the vision so they can join in on the journey.

Covering All the Bases

When communicating a vision, we want people not only to understand the vision but also to remember it—and then to communicate it to others. The most effective route into people's memory differs from person to person. Some people are visual learners, so we try to communicate the vision in a picture if we can. Other people are auditory learners, so we speak the vision over and over. There are also kinesthetic learners, so we try to incorporate things that people can do physically into communicating the vision.

Think also of including the head, heart, and hands in the communication. People need to understand the vision intellectually, mentally. They need to accept it emotionally and personally. They need to put it into action with their hands and feet. In terms of an organizational vision, people need to understand it, believe in it, and do it—head, heart, and hands.

As an example, consider an organization with five locations on three continents. During a concerted push to influence the culture and get everyone on board with the organization's vision, mission, and values, a plan was devised to work across geographic boundaries and bring the entire organization together. There were, of course, the predictable speeches, focus groups, posters, e-mail messages, and living room sessions. In addition, people at all five locations were invited to paint ceramic tiles to represent some part of the culture of the organization—its vision, mission, and values. It was an organizational bonding experience to come together and paint the tiles, and then the tiles were shared across geographic boundaries and mounted and displayed. Many people sent a tile to every location, and they still feel quite moved to contemplate that they have sent that gift to the other sites. Some have been able to travel to the other sites and see their contributions. This total consciousness-raising effort involved the head, the heart, and the hands.

Open a joint account. Connect the vision to real business outcomes if you lead a commercial enterprise or to tangible results and impact if you lead a nonprofit.

Keep to the FAQs. Employ technology, such as a knowledge base accessible through the Web or your organization's intranet, to answer questions from employees, customers, and stakeholders. Assign responsibility for responding.

Talk it up. Communicate, communicate, communicate. You cannot put your message out too often.

Back it up. If the message is out there, make sure people can see that it reflects real change. If they see one thing and hear another, your credibility is shot and your vision is dead.

Examples of Communicating a Vision

Effective leaders learn from example and experience. From the following instances, there are lessons to be drawn and ideas for action.

1. Keep the vision simple and easy to remember. When Nike coined the phrase "Just do it," these three words motivated its own staff even as they challenged the world to engage.

2. Tie the vision to specific and obvious organizational values. In 1939, Bill Hewlett and Dave Packard started a business in a garage. Over time, they created a way of doing business that came to be called the HP Way. It was an ideology that respected the individual, dedicated work to creating affordable quality and reliability, and carried a commitment to community responsibility.

3. Build meaning by giving individuals a personal connection to the vision. Mary Kay saw a way to enrich the lives of women not just through the use of cosmetic products but by making it possible for women to become entrepreneurs themselves.

4. Customize the benefits of the vision to each stakeholder group. Acknowledge the differences between them while making connections that show how all the pieces of the organization allow the vision to become reality. The U.S. Army's former slogan, Army of One, appealed to the individual soldier's needs and desires, highlighting individual strengths while connecting the soldier to the larger army organization.

5. Involve others and realize that a vision or mission can always grow and change. In the early days, Microsoft had a compelling mission: "a PC on every desk and in every home." Microsoft's mission propelled it for a long time, and it could be said that the company has achieved that mission. So what is Microsoft's mission today? "To help people and businesses throughout the world realize their full potential."

6. Make the vision attractive and motivating. Consider Google's mission of organizing the world's information and making it universally accessible and useful.

7. Walk the talk. CEO Herb Kelleher of Southwest Airlines took on the role of baggage carrier, flight attendant, and customer service agent a few times each year to stay abreast of the challenges his employees faced.

8. Make certain you demonstrate your belief in the vision. When former Chrysler chairman Lee Iacocca approached

the U.S. government seeking loans for a bailout, Congress was not impressed. But Iacocca had done his homework, and he argued that Chrysler's collapse would cost the country $2.75 billion in unemployment benefits alone. His speech convinced Congress to lend the money. Iacocca cut his own salary to $1 a year as a testament to his vision that Chrysler could turn around.

Meeting Resistance

In your efforts to communicate a vision, you may run into a couple of special situations. You may encounter resistance from your audience—or even from yourself. These circumstances increase the difficulty of your task, but fortunately, there are positive ways to work through them.

From Your Audience

One of the most important things any communicator ever learns is to design a message for the intended audience. It's natural to wish that your audience would be supportive, but if it is not, there's no point in pretending that it is. You must prepare your message for the audience you have. When listeners are resistant, it is often because there is a competing priority. Consider the following example.

A college's faculty members answered a written survey overwhelmingly indicating that they would be willing to give up their reserved parking places next to the building in order to be more egalitarian and less elitist. The idea was to give the best spaces to the students in an effort to be student centered. When faculty members continued using these spaces, the college president was frustrated. Even when he gave up his own parking space, the faculty continued to resist. Finally, after conducting some additional informal surveys on the golf course and in the cafeteria, the president realized that taking away the parking spaces would be taking away the only visible symbol the faculty members had of their importance and value to the college.

A person who is leading a change must overcommunicate—that is, communicate patiently again and again, on different levels, using different media. It is difficult and time consuming to lead people out of their resistance. The vision is distant and indistinct. The resistance is here and now. Overcommunication is one of the answers. It takes a stalwart leader to demonstrate the continuing patience needed to deal with resistance, and it takes a dynamic leader to engender the enthusiasm needed to lead people into the new vision. At the same time that the leader is patiently overcommunicating, he or she must start building the new, building the concrete part of the vision that the resistant audience can finally claim as its own.

The college president put numbered spaces at the far end of the parking lot and put up signs forbidding anyone except the owner of a space from parking there before 9:00 a.m. He had the "reserved" spaces near the building painted over, and he sent out a list of space assignments in the distant lot, based on seniority. The number one space (also the farthest from the building) was for the person who had been with the college the longest. Deans and directors got no additional consideration.

A dynamic leader is one who has a passion and talks about it frequently. In communicating a vision, this means not only talking about the intended result, but also speaking passionately about the process to get there. It may be a rather long time before some of the audience members get to the vision, but if they can buy into the process in the meantime, it will help move them along.

The college president and his executive staff came up with a mission statement about students' being the top priority, the maintenance team put up banners with the mission statement on them, and the student government started a nomination program to honor people who had gone "above and beyond." The president didn't talk about the parking issue any more. He got the newspaper to run a big ad about the new mission, and they followed it up with a feature article. People continued to joke about it, and some faculty members continued to come to work at 7:00 a.m. so they could get spaces next to the building, but slowly the problem diminished. And as it did, the enthusiasm for and pride in the new mission and vision increased.

Resistance shows up in unexpected ways. It's important to remember that it usually represents a competing priority and to figure out a way to address that priority. It's critical to keep communicating in as many ways as possible, and to be patient. Some people won't buy in until you've said it over and over, and when they finally do buy in, as far as they're concerned, that's the first time you've said it. So keep talking, patiently and passionately.

From Yourself

Sometimes you may find that you yourself are the one who is resistant. In this case, you are the one you need to work on. The time to intervene and try to change the vision to your own has passed. Maybe another opportunity will come in the future to influence the vision again, perhaps even next year. But in the meantime you really don't have a politically correct choice except to get on board. And it's very important how you phrase responses to questions if you don't agree. Make a list of sentences you'd feel okay saying:

✓ I'm fully on board with this, even though I'm still learning about it.

✓ I don't know everything about this yet, but I'm committed to it.

✓ I'm learning along with you guys, if I look a little confused, but I'm here with it.

It's very important *not* to say things that imply that you aren't on board:

✕ This wasn't really my idea, but let's give it a try until there's something better.

✕ I had a different plan, but this is what they said, so let's get on with it.

✕ I know this is stupid, but let's try to make the best of it, okay?

Even though you're still bringing yourself along, you need to model full commitment for your troops. It's hard for people to follow a leader who is not optimistic and hopeful about where they're going.

Last Words

You may have heard the saying that a person who does not read is no better off than a person who cannot read. It's much the same with vision statements. Having a vision but not communicating it isn't much of an improvement over not having a vision at all. A vision has to be shared in order to do the things it is meant to do: inspire, clarify, and focus the work of your organization.

Remember that as a leader, you're in the role of an early adopter. Your job is to communicate the vision to others in ways that will help them understand it, remember it, and then go on to share it themselves. In this way, the vision can become a bright lantern leading your organization toward its future.

Suggested Readings

Bridges, W. (2003). *Managing transitions: Making the most of change* (2nd ed.). Cambridge, MA: Perseus Publishing.

Denning, S. (2001). *The springboard: How storytelling ignites action in knowledge-era organizations*. Boston: Butterworth-Heinemann.

Gladwell, M. (2002). *The tipping point: How little things can make a big difference*. Boston: Back Bay Books.

Hughes, R. L., & Beatty, K. C. (2005). *Becoming a strategic leader: Your role in your organization's enduring success*. San Francisco: Jossey-Bass.

Lee, R. J., & King, S. N. (2001). *Discovering the leader in you: A guide to realizing your personal leadership potential*. San Francisco: Jossey-Bass.

Packard, D. (1995). *The HP way: How Bill Hewlett and I built our company*. New York: HarperBusiness.

Quigley, J. V. (1993). *Vision: How leaders develop it, share it, and sustain it*. New York: McGraw-Hill.

Background

CCL has studied the practice of leadership since 1970, and communicating a vision has been and continues to be a skill that leaders strive to develop. Our open-enrollment programs utilize assessments that have items directly related to a leader's ability to successfully communicate a vision, including a willingness to take risks, daring, and clear and effective communication. In a one-on-one coaching session, participants in our leadership development programs receive tools to become more effective at communicating vision. In addition, experiential activities that challenge leaders in the moment to cast a vision and receive peer feedback have set the foundation for the contents of this guidebook.

Key Point Summary

A vision is an imagined or discerned future state that clearly captures an organization's direction and defines its destination. One part of your job as a leader is to create commitment to your organization's vision. In order to do this, you have to communicate the vision effectively.

One way of communicating the vision is by telling a story. A story gives life to the vision, helps people see and remember it, and grounds it in common values and truths. If you don't have enough time to tell a story, you can use an elevator speech—a concise and convincing statement that communicates the vision in the amount of time of a typical elevator ride.

The more channels you open, the better your chances of communicating. Your organization's vision should be out front on its Web site, as well as on coffee mugs, T-shirts, pencils, notepads, and anything else that will keep it in the minds of employees, stakeholders, and customers.

Another effective strategy for communicating the vision is to engage others in one-on-one conversations. Personal connections give leaders opportunities to transmit information, receive feedback, build support, and create energy around the vision.

In your efforts to communicate the vision, you may encounter resistance from your audience. Resistance usually represents a competing priority, so it's important to figure out a way to address that priority. Keep communicating in as many ways as possible, and be patient. If you yourself are the one who is resistant, you are the one you need to work on. Even though you're still bringing yourself along, you need to model full commitment.

A vision has to be shared in order to do the things it is meant to do: inspire, clarify, and focus the work of your organization. Your job as a leader is to communicate the vision to others in ways that will help them understand it, remember it, and then go on to share it themselves.

Ordering Information

TO GET MORE INFORMATION, TO ORDER OTHER IDEAS INTO ACTION GUIDEBOOKS, OR TO FIND OUT ABOUT BULK-ORDER DISCOUNTS, PLEASE CONTACT US BY PHONE AT 336-545-2810 OR VISIT OUR ONLINE BOOKSTORE AT WWW.CCL.ORG/GUIDEBOOKS. PREPAYMENT IS REQUIRED FOR ALL ORDERS UNDER $100.

BECOMING A STRATEGIC LEADER: YOUR ROLE IN YOUR ORGANIZATION'S ENDURING SUCCESS

Richard L. Hughes and Katherine Colarelli Beatty
Jossey-Bass and Center for Creative Leadership, 2005
(CCL Stock No. 2174)

Today's organizations face difficult challenges in order to remain competitive—the quickening pace of change, increasing uncertainty, growing ambiguity, and complexity. To meet these challenges, organizations must broaden the scope of leadership responsibility for strategic leadership and engage more people in the process of leadership.

In *Becoming a Strategic Leader* Richard Hughes and Katherine Beatty from the Center for Creative Leadership (CCL) offer executives and managers a handbook for implementing a strategic leadership process that reaches leaders at all levels of organizations.

Based on CCL's successful Developing the Strategic Leader program, this book outlines the framework of strategic leadership and contains practical suggestions on how to develop the individual, team, and organizational skills needed for institutions to become more adaptable, flexible, and resilient. The authors also show how individual managers can exercise effective strategic leadership through their distinctive and systemic approach—thinking, acting, and influencing.

DISCOVERING THE LEADER IN YOU: A GUIDE TO REALIZING YOUR PERSONAL LEADERSHIP POTENTIAL

Robert J. Lee and Sara N. King
Jossey-Bass and Center for Creative Leadership, 2001
(CCL Stock No. 2067)

This book is based on a simple, obvious point: leadership roles should be filled by people who deliberately decide they want to be in them. Yet many executives and managers find that they have become leaders by default rather than as a result of a personal choice. In fact, a great many people drift into or away from being leaders simply because they have not done the work of matching their own honestly described self with the realities of the leadership role. Not until they are well into their careers do many individuals seriously explore their personal fit for leadership. But by then, it is often too late to prepare for more gratifying roles or to get out of situations that don't make sense for them as individuals.

Discovering the Leader in You offers a planful approach to understanding how aspects of personality, character, vision, home life, values, and skills match with essential leadership activities. This unique system of self-discovery clearly shows what it looks like to fit or not to fit in leadership roles in organizations.

This book will help executives, managers, and potential leaders—seasoned veterans and those considering leading as a new direction in their careers—to gain more personal insight into what leadership really means to them, to retain more control over their career choices, and consequently to achieve more personal success as leaders.

TO ORDER THESE BOOKS, VISIT OUR ONLINE BOOKSTORE AT WWW.CCL.ORG/PUBLICATIONS.

The articles in LiA *give me insight into the various aspects of leadership and how they can be applied in my work setting.*

Clayton H. Osborne
Vice President, Human Resources
Bausch & Lomb

LiA *sparks ideas that help me better understand myself as a leader, both inside and outside the organization.*

Kenneth Harris
Claims Director
Scottsdale Insurance Company

Leadership in Action

*A publication of the
Center for Creative Leadership
and Jossey-Bass*

Leadership in Action is a bimonthly publication that aims to help practicing leaders and those who train and develop practicing leaders by providing them with insights gained in the course of CCL's educational and research activities. It also aims to provide a forum for the exchange of information and ideas between practitioners and CCL staff and associates.

To order, please contact Customer Service, Jossey-Bass, 989 Market Street, San Francisco, CA 94103-1741. Telephone: 888/378-2537; fax: 415/951-8553. See the Jossey-Bass Web site, at www.josseybass.com.